Nature's Children

GOPHERS

Jen Green

GROLIER

FACTS IN BRIEF

Classification of Gophers

Class: *Mammalia* (mammals)
Order: *Rodentia* (rodents)
Suborder: *Sciuromorpha* (squirrel-like rodents)
Family: *Geomyidae* (pocket gophers)
Species: 40 species divided into 6 genera and two tribes: western and eastern pocket gophers.

World distribution.   North and Central America.

Habitat.   Varied, including deserts, scrublands, grasslands, alpine meadows, and tropical lowlands.

Distinctive physical characteristics.   Medium-sized rodents with prominent incisors, large-clawed feet, and short, bare tails. Fur-lined cheek pouches give the group its name.

Habits.   Gophers spend much of their lives below ground, but also come above ground to find food, which they carry in their cheek pouches. These solitary rodents do not hibernate.

Diet.   Roots, bulbs, and tubers in the soil, leafy parts above ground.

© 2004 The Brown Reference Group plc
Printed and bound in U.S.A.
Edited by John Farndon and Angela Koo

Published by:

GROLIER

An imprint of Scholastic
Library Publishing
Old Sherman Turnpike, Danbury,
Connecticut 06816

Library of Congress Cataloging-in-Publication Data
Green, Jen.
  Gophers / Jen Green.
    p. cm. — (Nature's children)
  Summary: Describes the physical characteristics, habits, and natural environment of gophers.
  ISBN 0–7172–5957–9 (set)   —   ISBN 0–7172–5966–8
    1. Pocket gophers—Juvenile literature. [1. Gophers.] I. Title. II. Series.

QL737.R654H36 2004
599.36′5—dc22

          2003049174

Contents

Pocket gophers churn up lots of soil as they burrow through the ground.

Out in the yard on a sunny morning, you may come upon a strange sight: small heaps of fresh earth on a neatly trimmed lawn. This is a sight that all gardeners dread—a sign that gophers have moved in.

Gophers are burrowing creatures that spend much of their lives underground. A variety of other digging animals are also called gophers, including mud turtles and salamanders. However, true gophers are furry creatures more correctly called pocket gophers. So where are a gopher's pockets? On its head, for they are fur-lined cheek pouches that are used to carry food.

Pocket gophers are found only in the Americas. Elsewhere small heaps of earth in gardens are usually a sign of moles. Farmers view gophers as pests because they nibble crops. Gardeners dislike them because they ruin lawns and flower beds. However, gophers can actually help farmers by making the soil more fertile.

The World of Rodents

Opposite page:
Capybaras are gophers' biggest cousins. They live in South America and are almost as big as pigs.

Gophers belong to a huge group of animals called rodents. There are more than 1,700 different kinds of rodent. Rats, mice, voles, and gerbils are all rodents. So are agoutis, guinea pigs, and porcupines. All rodents have two pairs of long, sharp teeth called incisors at the front of their jaws. They use them to nibble and gnaw on plant food. The word rodent comes from a Latin word meaning "to gnaw."

Rodents are hardy survivors. They are found on every continent except Antarctica and in every type of terrain from icy tundra to hot deserts. Rodents breed quickly. They are seen as pests when they invade stored grain. Rodents such as rats spread disease.

There are three main families of rodents. Rats and mice make up the largest group. The other two groups are cavies, which include guinea pigs and chinchillas, and squirrels. Gophers are members of the squirrel group.

The Squirrel Clan

Squirrels are one of the best-known groups of rodents. More than 370 different kinds of squirrel-like rodents are found around the world. Experts divide them into two main groups: tree-dwelling squirrels and ground squirrels. Tree-dwellers are dainty and graceful as they leap through the branches. Ground squirrels are generally stockier than their tree-dwelling cousins, with shorter tails. Gophers are ground squirrels.

The ground squirrel clan includes prairie dogs, which live together in vast burrows called towns. It also includes groundhogs, which spend the whole winter asleep. Bold chipmunks steal tidbits from picnic sites. Susliks are desert-dwelling ground squirrels. Marmots live high on mountains, while beavers nest in rafts of sticks in lakes. With 34 species gophers are quite a large group of ground squirrels. Pocket mice are the only other group with cheek pouches to carry food.

Opposite page: *This golden-mantled squirrel is a ground squirrel like gophers. It lives in forests in the mountains of western North America.*

Gopher Country

Pocket gophers are found only in North and Central America. The gopher clan is divided into two groups called tribes. One tribe lives on the western side of the continent, the other on the east. The western tribe inhabits a huge region stretching from Saskatchewan and Manitoba in Canada southward all the way to Mexico and Panama. Eastern pocket gophers inhabit the central and eastern United States. However, few gophers live on the rolling plains and croplands of the midwestern United States.

Gopher country can be any kind of terrain where the soil is soft enough to tunnel through. However, gophers keep mainly to open country or sparsely wooded areas where tree roots don't get in the way below ground. Some types of gophers inhabit deserts and scrubland; others prefer grasslands. Yet other species colonize mountain meadows up to 13,000 feet (4,000 meters). They can live above the timberline, beyond which no trees grow.

Botta's pocket gophers belong to the western tribe.
They live in the southwestern U.S.

*Pocket gophers have very short and squat bodies—
ideal for crawling along tunnels.*

Shapes and Sizes

Gophers are shy creatures that are rarely seen above ground. However, you may be lucky enough to glimpse one shoveling earth out of its burrow or squatting nearby, nibbling plants. Pocket gophers are medium-sized, stout rodents measuring 5-12 inches (12-30 centimeters) long. Males are larger than females and may be up to twice as big. Gophers are chunky rodents with no visible neck and a short, bare tail.

A gopher's whole body is suited to digging and its underground lifestyle. Its front limbs are strong and muscular. The front paws, used as shovels, are broad with large claws. The long, strong incisor teeth are also used for digging. You can often see them poking out in front of their lips. The gopher's eyes and ears are small. They can be closed tightly when the animal is digging so earth doesn't get in.

A Furry Coat

Like other rodents, gophers have a thick, furry coat covering almost every part of their body. Only the tail and feet have fewer hairs and look bare. Gopher fur is generally brown, but the exact shade varies from dark to pale and sandy to reddish. The rodent's fur color usually matches the soil where it lives. That helps it hide from enemies.

The gopher's fur is soft and fine, so it doesn't get clogged with wet soil. It can be smoothed in any direction. That helps the gopher back down its burrow without getting stuck. The skin is loose, which helps gophers squeeze into tight spaces and turn around quickly. All these features help these rodents be quick and nimble in their underground world.

A gopher's fur looks fluffy because it can be smoothed in any direction to move through tunnels.

Tooth and Claw

A gopher's main digging tools are its front paws with their long claws. A fringe of stiff hairs around the edge of each paw makes it even more effective at scooping earth. When a tunneling gopher hits a tough tree root, it gnaws right through it with its sharp incisors. These long, chisel-shaped teeth stick out beyond its lips, so the rodent can close its mouth when digging. That helps keep dirt from getting into its mouth.

You might think a gopher's teeth and claws would get worn away with all that digging. But unlike human teeth, a gopher's teeth never stop growing. Nor do its claws, so they never get blunt. A gopher's teeth and claws grow an amazing 1/16 of an inch (1 millimeter) in just one day. That helps keep them sharp and strong.

Opposite page: *The gopher's long, chisel-shaped teeth are great for gnawing through any tree root that blocks its way underground.*

Tale of a Tail

The gopher's tail does not look like much compared to those of most other rodents. Tree squirrels have thick, bushy tails that help them balance as they dart through the treetops. Among ground squirrels water-loving beavers have broad tails that act as paddles. Desert-dwelling Cape ground squirrels have long, plumy tails that they use as sunshades. Compared to these fine tails, the gopher's is short, stubby, and almost hairless.

However, even the gopher's tail is useful. With their thick, furry coats rodents cannot cool down in hot weather by sweating, as humans do. The gopher's bare tail helps it lose body heat. Gophers in warm regions have longer tails than their cousins in cooler places. The bare tail is also very sensitive to touch. When running backward along its burrow, the gopher holds its tail just above the earth and uses it to feel the way.

Sensing the World

Like other animals, pocket gophers rely on their keen senses to find out about the world around them. The gopher's senses are finely tuned to help it avoid its enemies and seek out food and a mate. These little rodents have the same five main senses that you have: sight, hearing, smell, taste, and touch.

A keen sense of smell helps the rodent find food by day or night. Above ground, sight may help a gopher spot an enemy, but it is little use in a dark burrow.

When the gopher is below ground, hearing, scent, and also touch are more important than sight. Gophers have long whiskers on their snouts and special sensitive hairs in the fur all over their bodies. When danger threatens, a combination of several senses often helps gophers gain the split second of time they need to make a quick getaway.

Deadly Enemies

Gophers have many enemies in the wild, including mammals such as foxes, coyotes, badgers, and weasels. Birds such as owls and hawks swoop down from above to pounce on unwary gophers. Snakes such as rattlers also view the rodents as a nourishing snack.

A gopher's burrow is its main defense against all these enemies. The first hint of danger will send a gopher that is searching for food above ground scrambling for the safety of its hole. Gophers normally plug their burrow entrances with earth to keep out intruders. Snakes are among the few predators able to chase a gopher down its burrow. If the rodent senses a snake in pursuit, it will quickly scrabble at the soil to make its tunnel collapse. That usually stops the snake in its tracks.

Rattlesnakes are among the gopher's most deadly enemies. They may even chase a gopher down its burrow.

Home Sweet Home

There's no place like home for gophers, just like many other animals. A gopher's home is a network of tunnels covering 2,000 square feet (180 meters) or more. This underground dwelling provides not only safety from predators but also protection from heat, cold, and storms.

A gopher's home contains two different kinds of burrows. Long tunnels running just below the surface are used for feeding. Many gophers extend them regularly to reach new food sites. At a deeper level, up to 6 feet (2 meters) below ground, the rodent digs its permanent quarters. There is a nesting chamber lined with soft grass where the gopher sleeps, a larder where it stores food, and a toilet chamber, which helps keep the rest of the burrow clean. After all that digging some gophers spend the rest of their lives in just one burrow. Others move on in search of fresh feeding grounds or a mate.

Busy Burrowers

With their sharp claws and teeth gophers can dig new feeding tunnels amazingly quickly. A busy gopher can make half a dozen holes in your lawn in a single night! The digging rodent first shovels soil under its body. It then turns around and heaves it up to the surface between its chest and forepaws. Above ground, gophers leave mounds of loose soil shaped like crescents or horseshoes around their holes. Regular, cone-shaped mounds, which resemble miniature volcanoes, are more likely to be the work of prairie dogs or moles.

In the wild, gophers tend to live more closely together in areas where plant food is abundant. Food-rich areas may contain up to 100 rodents per acre (240 per hectare). Places where food is scarce have fewer rodents.

As well as gophers themselves, a variety of other creatures may shelter in gopher burrows. They include insects, lizards, mice, and rabbits, and in dry areas, burrowing owls.

A Bite to Eat

Most types of animals are either carnivores (meat eaters) or herbivores (plant eaters). Like other rodents, gophers are firmly in the plant-eater camp. They feed mainly below ground on the nourishing roots and bulbs they come across while tunneling. Above ground, they nibble stems and leaves of wild plants, crops, and also tree bark. A little ring of turf around their entrance holes may be nibbled short and neat.

As well as long incisors, gophers also have sturdy, rounded teeth called molars farther back in their jaws. These strong grinding teeth make short work of even the toughest plants. Gophers get almost all the moisture they need from the plants they eat, so they rarely need to drink water. In desert areas the rodents nibble juicy cactus plants when water is scarce.

Opposite page: There are few things a gopher likes more than to sit in the entrance to its burrow gnawing on a lump of tree bark.

Finding Food

We humans are active during the day and rest at night. Gophers follow a different rhythm—they are partly nocturnal (night-active). Their senses are suited to their gloomy burrows, so they don't mind the dark.

On pitch-black nights when few enemies are around, they leave their holes to search for food in the open. When they find a good food source, they quickly stuff their cheek pouches, using nimble fingers. The fur-lined pouches in their cheeks stretch back as far as their shoulders. Back in the safety of the burrow, they turn these "pockets" inside out to remove all the tidbits. Special cheek muscles pull the pouches back into shape once the gopher has emptied its pockets.

This gopher has stuffed its cheek pockets so full of leaves that it looks like a little fur ball.

Winter Survival

Many ground squirrels aren't out and about in winter. Prairie dogs, groundhogs, and marmots all spend the winter in a deep sleep called hibernation. In fact, groundhogs are famous for emerging from their winter slumber at the same time every year.

Gophers are different. They remain active through the winter, though in the very worst weather they don't go out much. Like many rodents, they may put in a store of food to last through the worst days. However, a flurry of snow doesn't prevent them from leaving their burrows. After a heavy snowfall they come above ground and tunnel through the snow to nibble tree bark. They sometimes bring up soil to line these snowy burrows. When the snow melts, just the earthen linings, called "gopher cores," are left on the grass.

Opposite page: *Gopher cores are the earthy linings of the burrows gophers make under the winter snow. When the snow melts in spring, you can often see gopher cores crisscrossing the ground.*

Keep Off My Patch!

Opposite page:
A gopher does not welcome visitors. If another gopher strays onto its patch, it bares its teeth and squeals.

Are you naturally sociable, or do you like spending time on your own? Some types of ground squirrels, such as prairie dogs and marmots, are "social"—they live together in a big group. Not gophers. They are "solitary," which means they spend almost all their lives on their own.

Do you have a private corner where you keep your own things, where visitors are welcome only with your permission? Many types of animals have a territory—a private patch where they feed, rest, or breed, and which they defend against others of their kind. Gophers are very territorial and get very cross if another gopher enters their burrow. The burrow owner tries to scare the intruder away by baring its teeth and making fierce noises. If neither animal backs down, a fight breaks out. The squabble may end in serious injury, or when the winner chases the loser off the patch.

Mating Time

No matter how fierce and solitary animals are by nature, they must come together to mate so that a new generation can be born. During the breeding season gophers bury their differences as the mating instinct takes over. Each rodent usually keeps to its own burrow; but at mating time these barriers break down, and males and females nest together. After mating, the male returns to his own territory. The female is left to raise the young on her own.

Many animals time their matings so that the young will be born when the weather is warm, and food is plentiful. Gophers instinctively know to do this too. In cool places they usually breed in early spring, so the babies will emerge at a time when there is plenty of plant food. In dry places gophers breed in the rainy season. However in warm, moist regions with lush vegetation gophers mate at any time of year.

Opposite page: Spring is a time of plentiful food for gophers. So that is when they look to start a family.

The Babies Are Born

Opposite page:
It's spring, and this mother gopher is just about to go underground to give birth to her young.

Gophers are renowned as quick breeders. Females usually give birth to between three and six young in a litter (group of offspring). In cool regions gopher moms give birth just once a year, but in warm places they can give birth to several litters yearly. When you realize that these babies may start to breed themselves within a few months, you'll understand why gophers spell trouble when they move into your neighborhood!

The young of large mammals such as deer and horses spend many months developing in their mother's womb before they are born. This time is called gestation. In smaller species such as gophers gestation time is much shorter. Young gophers are born just 18 or 19 days after their mom and dad mated. Like all mammals, they feed on their mother's milk, a very nourishing food.

This baby is an Arctic ground squirrel, a cousin of the gopher. It lives in the far North.

Growing Up

Gophers grow up very fast compared to larger mammals such as monkeys and dolphins. Humans take the longest time of all. Newborn gophers are pink and hairless, but their fur begins to grow after a few days. At birth their eyes and ears are tightly closed, so they cannot see or hear; but the eyes and ears open after about three weeks.

By the age of about one month old the babies start to eat plant food. But they soon learn to be independent of the mother. About two months after birth the young gophers leave the nest to start life on their own. They usually leave on dark nights to avoid being seen by predators. They may have to travel some way above ground before they find a suitable burrow site. Then they dig down and move in. In the wild, gophers can live up to six years, but many get killed by predators before they reach one year old.

Pesky Rodents

People have seen gophers as pests since settlers began to tame the wild lands of North America. Farmers say the rodents cause millions of dollars of damage by nibbling the roots and leafy parts of crops. Ranchers say they spoil their pastures. Yet gophers are sometimes blamed for damage caused by the trampling feet of cattle. Horses and also cattle have been known to trip in gopher burrows and break their legs.

Gophers are also unpopular when they move into built-up areas. In gardens they dig up flower bulbs, munch prize vegetables, and damage fruit trees. Sometimes they gnaw through sprinkler systems. Many a neat lawn has been ruined by the little rodents. All over America farmers, ranchers, and gardeners have declared war on the little pests!

War on Gophers

Once gophers have moved onto your property, they are very difficult to get rid of. People have tried all kinds of methods to wipe out the little rodents, often with little success. Gardeners sometimes bury chicken wire to protect their fruit trees, but the rodents just burrow under it. People have tried to smoke gophers out using poison gas, but the rodents seal off the poisoned tunnels with earth.

In days gone by, farmers used to flood their fields in spring to get rid of gophers. The rodents were forced to leave their burrows or drown, but they often came back once the floods had gone. Farmers have also used barn owls to hunt the rodents, but the owls often move on before killing all the gophers in one area. Traps and poisoned bait are the most effective means of controlling gophers. Yet people find that unless the rodents are wiped out completely, the survivors breed quickly and soon replace those that have died.

Opposite page:
To keep gopher numbers down, farmers sometimes encourage barn owls to nest. Barn owls hunt gophers and kill them.

Live and Let Live

In recent years experts have started to realize that the natural world is often more complicated than was once thought. Gophers can be helpful as well as harmful. They nibble farmers' crops, yet can also help improve farm soil. Gopher burrows allow air and water into the ground, which increases fertility. Their droppings and the plants they bury enrich the soil, which helps crops grow.

On ranches gopher burrows help loosen soil packed down by the feet of cattle. The rodents also provide food for wild hunters such as foxes, hawks, and owls. Maybe it's time we learned to live with gophers instead of trying to destroy them. After all, gophers lived in America's wild places long before humans got here. Long may they continue to enjoy the wide open spaces—only, please, stay out of my backyard!

Words to Know

Gestation The period between mating and birth, during which young mammals develop inside their mother.

Herbivore An animal that eats mainly plants.

Hibernation A state of deep sleep that lasts many weeks. It helps animals survive the winter.

Incisors The sharp, chisel-shaped teeth at the front of mammals' jaws. Rodents use their long incisors to gnaw plant food.

Litter A group of young all born to a mother at one time.

Mammal Any warm-blooded animal that is covered by hair or fur, gives birth to live young, and makes milk to feed them.

Nocturnal An animal that is mainly active at night.

Predator An animal that hunts other creatures for food. Animals that are hunted for food are known as prey.

Rodent One of a group of mammals with long front teeth called incisors. The group of rodents includes rats and mice.

Social An animal that lives with others of its kind in a cooperative group.

Territory An area where an animal hunts or breeds. The animal generally defends its territory against other animals.

Timberline The zone on a mountain beyond which the climate is too cold for trees to grow.

INDEX

Cover Photo: Corbis: Gunter Marx Photography
Photo Credits: Ardea: John Cancalosi 12, Chris Harvey 19; Bruce Coleman: Bruce Coleman Inc. 15, Natural Selection Inc. 8; Corbis: Niall Benvie 44, John Conrad 23, Raymond Gehman 43, George D. Lepp 4, Joe McDonald 28, Bill Ross 36, Kennan Ward 39; Getty Images/Imagebank: Paul McCormick 40; NHPA: Norbert Wu 16; Nature Picture Library: Jeff Foott 31; Oxford Scientific Films: Jeff Foott 32, Jeff Foott/OKAPIA 20; Science Photo Library: Tom McHugh 26/27, 35, Joe Sartore 11; Still Pictures: David Hoffman 7.